HURRY BACK

HURRY BACK

poems by
Alvin Greenberg

LOST HORSE PRESS

Sandpoint · Idaho

ACKNOWLEDGMENTS

Agni Review: elegy in blue and white

Chelsea: holy wars; the search for a unified theory; quotidian; wintering over at the end of the century; against dreaming; happiness; i wish i knew america better; the man in the moon

Cincinnati Poetry Review: the barges at night on the ohio river

Colorado Review: crystal night; last things; almost always

Crosscurrents: the art of the possible

Gettysburg Review: freight train, freight train; hurry back; something amazing; what with; leakage; in the graveyard, my father; true believer

Georgia Review: plate tectonics

Marlboro Review: optical illusions; killer asteroids

Minnesota Review: a loss for words

Nimrod: thanacopia

Ohio Review: starlight, starbright . . .

Quarterly West: crossing central illinois

Shenandoah: shadows

Tar River Poetry: bad weather

"the search for a unified theory," "quotidian," "wintering over at the end of the century," "against dreaming," "happiness," and "i wish i knew america better" received the Chelsea Award for Poetry; "thanacopia" was the winner of the Pablo Neruda Award.

My thanks to The Loft, the National Endowment for the Arts, and Macalester College for, respectively, a Loft-McKnight Award, an Individual Artists Fellowship, and a sabbatical extension grant, all of which helped support the completion of this collection.

First Edition

Cover Art: Robert Meier
Author Photo: Robert Meier
Book Design: Christine Holbert

LIBRARY OF CONGRESS CATALOGING-IN-PUBLICATION DATA

Greenberg, Alvin.
Hurry back : poems / by Alvin Greenberg.
     p. cm.
I. Title.
PS3557.R377H87 2005
811'.54—dc22

          2005001521

BOOKS BY ALVIN GREENBERG

POETRY

Why We Live With Animals

Heavy Wings

And Yet

In/Direction

Metaform

Dark Lands

The House of the Would-Be Gardener

The Metaphysical Giraffe

SHORT STORIES

How the Dead Live

The Man in the Cardboard Mask

Delta q

The Discovery of America & Other Tales of Terror

NOVELS

Time Lapse

The Invention of the West

Going Nowhere

The Small Waves

NONFICTION

The Dog of Memory: A Family Album of Secrets and Silences

CONTENTS

III. HURRY BACK

for Janet, who gave me both a title and a reason

Life is not a mystery.

—*Ortega y Gasset*

I. THANACOPIA

1. cincinnati

> I like trees because they seem more resigned to
> the way they have to live than other things do.
>
> —*Willa Cather*

i mean to visit the cemetery again
that i've not been back to since my father's funeral,
and i mean to go there in humid august
when that late summer ohio valley heat
hammers you into the earth like an angry gravedigger
and dares you to move on, to take one step
out of the sycamore shade. i will squat down,
sweating, and stay there among those generations
until my shirt's soaked and my legs ache
and the sun slides in under the pale branches
and their wide, five-fingered leaves and i remember,
when the evening brings no relief, that
in another cemetery, on the western side of town,
under trees i've never seen, my mother lies.
there i mean to go in another kind of weather:
the winter rain that greys these skies for weeks on end
when the trees have nothing left to give you shelter,
the weather you're left out in all alone
while black umbrellas huddle around a distant grave,
not the weather i thought of when i was a child
reading about explorers 'braving the storm,' but
weather of no excitement, not the weather of armies,
not the weather you dare to hunker down in,
but the weather of abandonment,
rain always on the edge of becoming ice.

2. savannah

SLOW:
YOU ARE
RESPONSIBLE
FOR YOUR OWN WAKE

—sign in ship channel

even history takes a dim view of history
with its cords of bodies stacked behind the house,
and there is no future in the future, that
fast growing pulpwood thicket waiting
to be harvested. nothing to do in the meantime
except settle down on some old stump
back of the paper mill beside the stinking pond
and tell sad stories of the deaths of kings
because that's all that we can do, all we
have ever done. this place is titled 'in memoriam'
and all its stories begin with 'once upon a time'
and end 'when this you see remember me.'
that's the secret formula, the only one we have,
and everyone knows it, even if they have doubts,
which few do and not for long. slow, slow:
nothing's given away here, and though everything's,
finally, taken, including today, this very today
which is the only today we're ever going to have,
none of us here struck the match that said so.
we just build, slowly, beneath the live oaks,
a little shelter for it, carefully,
with our own hands, from whatever scraps
we've cherished, a kind of elegaic lean-to,
set right out in the weather because the weather's
what there is and where we do our loving.

3. st. paul

Who feels enough confidence to say anything?
All I know is that no matter what we have
dreamed or desired it slips away unless by a
supreme effort we struggle to detain it.

—*W.C. Williams*

at first she only came back to him in his dreams.
then she took form, and the form was everywhere,
rising out of the earth, stretching, making
a landscape out of nothing wherever it appeared.
he wanted to be constable or the watercolor turner.
he wanted, he wanted. . . . there is a giant oak
in the woodbury united methodist church cemetery
that also has its wants, and the earth: the earth
that neither wants nor asks nor demands but gets,
eventually, everything.
          at first she only came back
to him in his dreams: a postcard from a museum,
a phone call, a brief encounter in a london teashop,
worlds without weather that he always woke from.
now, when he gets there, snow covers the stones,
his path a weaving furrow quickly filling in,
but the infallible oak is there to point the way
with its longest, lowest branch. he listens.
he has questions. the articulate landscape
won't deny him: that much he's learned to trust.
the wind is a strict old companion. he kneels
in the snow, his back to its complaints.
            at first
she only came back to him in his dreams. more
than enough, he thought, those brief benedictions.
then she took form, and the form was everywhere.

4. silver bay

> Where, in what heavenly gardens, in what trees,
> from what lovingly unsheathed flower-calyxes
> do the strange fruits of consolation ripen?
>
> —*Rilke*

i read in the guide book that eden, like san francisco,
is built on a fault line, but i did not read how not
to go there. city of songs. in the old days they put
the cemeteries outside the city walls, and people like you
and i put on the duke's uniform, took up his weapons,
so we could do guard duty on those narrow ramparts
where the night winds blew first this way, then that,
and balanced between love and loss we learned the songs
they sang there, which are all the songs there are:

     when one we love has gone away

     it's only memory that preserves, they say.

     well, memory preserves, that's true,

     but they forget it works both ways: the you

     my memory preserves, preserves me, too.
now: i walk the strip of pebbled beach beside the lake
watching the fog drift in, feeling it dampen my skin
while the sun in the hills behind me tries to push it back.
the wind in the balsams has no more sense of direction
than i do. there are places i need to go to where i can't
stay. such songs we have to sing, and all with the same
name. at first in my dreams, but didn't she really come
walking down the beach under a wide hat, pants rolled,
shirt untucked, bending to pick a lake superior agate up?
once upon a time: once upon a time, i begin, once upon
a time we strolled this narrow line along the shore while
agates flowered underfoot and everything was understood.

oh i have left my home
and all my companions are sleepers
and the quiet of the ladybug and the white clouds

—*Wendy Parrish*, "Melody in Burghley Field"

has everyone except teenagers given up going to cemeteries?
and we know what they're there for: toppling the stones
or fucking behind them, howling like ghosts in each others' ears,

no more aware of what they're sinking to in that soft ground
than my dog when i take her running through roselawn cemetery,
skipping over markers set flush in the grass, thinking:

the quick and the dead, only a thin layer of earth between us.
there's not a lot we can do for the dead but water their stones.
put their names up in lights on the marquee of our memory.

but i remember how my parents' generation used to visit: sundays,
afternoons, planning the drive, dressing up, cutting flowers,
easing into and out of those big old cars. paying their respects

was what they said. and they strolled among grey headstones
so slowly they might have imagined themselves mirror images
to their loved ones barely moving on the other side of the lawn:

mom and dad here: sole to sole with mom and dad below. the words
they had were mostly for themselves. i talk to you. knowing
how little there really is to say, i wander between these

generations, frozen as my father, passionate as the kids.
it's early wednesday morning. i love you. the snow shows me
what a straight line i've made from the gate in the fence to this
blue granite stone that tells me more than i need to know.

the only other footprints belong to birds and squirrels and rabbits.
this is not visiting weather. how do we do this in a time

when this isn't much done anymore? i wish someone were watching,
someone to say, yes, we still do this. but even the church
which i never enter is dark. what isn't ritual is ours alone

to carry out. i have seen the sun set and the sun rise here.
this morning it burns low, a cold candle in the snow clouds.
the little dog waits in the car. i wish there were ladybugs

to keep us company. i brought one flower: take me, take me.

when i learned to walk in the dark
it was the darkest night in the history
of the universe. someone had thrown a blanket
over the moon. others had switched off
the stars. the streetlights were in collusion
with all this, and who could blame them?
not a light in a window, on a porch.
i got out of bed and took my first steps into
the dark. i left my glasses on the nightstand.
why was i even awake, you may ask.
it was the hour, i awoke on the hour,
or the hour and a half, whenever grim routine
put its hand on my shoulder and shook me.
so i said ok and got up and this time
left my glasses on the nightstand because
i had seen this done once and marveled at it
and figured that it was my turn now
since the night had nothing to offer
but a knotted darkness no optician yet had
ground and polished our vision to unravel.
and lo and behold, i knew where the bedroom
door was, i knew where the stairs were,
i found the kitchen sink and i thought,
as long as i'm here why not have a drink
of water, and i did, the glass rising
from the plastic drainer into my hand,
and the faucet an offering, the water, too,
falling right into the glass, not even
wetting my fingers, and i drank and it was
cold like my bare feet on the linoleum
floor. and i looked out the windows:
west where as always the last light had gone

and east where no light was coming
for many hours yet and north, too, where
i had sometimes seen the aurora borealis,
once as if i were standing under a heavenly
shower pouring watery blue-green light
over my head and shoulders, because this
was far north, and winter, but there was
of course no aurora borealis, not that
night. so i gulped down the rest of my water
and rinsed the cold glass and set it back
on the drainer and went back to bed,
my feet on the bare wooden steps, my hand
sliding up the banister. i drifted
through the bedroom door, i floated
back into the bed, i never saw a thing,
but the pillow welcomed my head and the thick
covers settled back over me, i felt their weight
and i was soon warm, reaching out
at the very last, just before darkness
claimed me entirely, to touch my glasses
lightly where they lay on the nightstand,
patted them like a good dog who'd sleep
beside my bed all night, waiting till
morning and time to be taken out again.

how carefully, carefully, you carry the cup of coffee
across the living room carpet to the couch, aware
every taut step of the way how it wants to leap out.
you don't say "trip," you don't say "spill," you don't
believe that words can empty the precious containers
of your world, you just don't want to chance things
getting an edge on you, you want to sit on the couch,
sip that coffee ever so carefully, and read the morning
paper while the dogs you've just let out putter around
the backyard, peeing here, peeing there, and the blood
on your neck where you cut yourself shaving autographs
your white collar with the body's indelible signature.

seepage from the inside out: it never stops. or this:
when it does, everything else will stop too. meanwhile,
the flood: passionate magma easing up hot and heavy
through earth's crust's cracks and crannies, spreading,
cooling, solidifying into what we'll live with forever
after. and all the liquids that like the buckets we are
we carry around inside us: that most of what we are,
moist, watery, clotted, thin and red, pale and viscous,
the self's soggy volume that we wrap ourselves around,
forever ready to leak away at the first sharp poke. tell
a dry tale and who'll believe it? the desert itself's
a story of open pores, leaky flasks. the one sound we
all know is the drip drip drip of the infernal faucet.

oh, springwater, treesap, heartstuff, this bubbling up
of language: once it's out, we know where it's going.
when my mother died my father fled. was the air let out
of his life? then he wanted out too. and the bottles
he took, the bottles he bought, found, cadged, or stole,

released their contents on his behalf as well: the way
everything wants out: the tears of his telling, the only
ones i ever saw. weeping, the uncle who brought him back.

freud was wrong about the death wish: it's just the self
like everything else wanting to flee its sad container.
it's only the others gripping our wrists or ankles that
keeps us all from slipping through the cracks. and then
there's time: that widening hole even they can't hold us
back from. slowly, layers of subcutaneous fat leak away
and the face caves in, its hills and valleys turning soft
and brown as an aging landscape, like earth itself spied
from above, pocked and lumpy as it goes spinning away:
a drop, a drop, hung on the lip of the faucet. and then.

because everything wants to go back where it came from:
rain to the wide, flat lakes, cooled magma to sink under
its own weight back into the depths again, the dying to
their toys, to oldcountry languages they never even spoke.
perhaps freud was wrong again, the womb merely incidental,
and we shuttle back and forth in our lives like migratory
birds: no one place can hold us. the world is a sieve.
the year is a sieve. the lives of others are sieves we
fall through just as we fall through the sieves of our
own porous lives. not even the fine mesh of these lines,
from which we expect so much, can finally hold us in.

this is my last will and testament, full
of sound mind and signatures. little cash. i
am going, going. few possessions. gone,
like small smoke in this nasty, wet, west wind,
just a puff of pollen from these hill country junipers
bringing a brief, funereal twinge to nose or eye
(though like death they're only busy propagating).

stay here long enough and you become allergic
to such things. but no one stays that long. i
have only a few words to leave behind. the wind
will soon take them. fine. we're little chimneys,
all of us, the dark ash of our lives rising
right up through us till there's nothing left
but teeth and bone and a few bright rings for

the nazi wind to pick over. the will to survive
is no doubt a good thing, like a campfire,
the wood wet, the cold always at your back. but i
had no idea what it was like. in the end
no one does. that's what lawyers are for, why
there's a form for this, a windy ritual of
dispersal to gather around, the fire sputtering,

the scrawl witnessed, the t crossed, the dotted i.

the barges at night on the ohio river

are invisible, though there's some sense of presence
in the unlit quarter mile between the blinking yellow
bow light and the white light at the stern of the tug,
something more than just that heavy throb of twin diesels
pushing the high-riding, empty string upstream.

the river grows a little darker as they pass, a tow
five barges long and three across, slow against
the current, seen, for awhile, from the kentucky side,
backlit against the downtown cincinnati glitter,
like some gigantic spaceship crossing the starry sky,

a blankness in the plenisphere at first, black hole
that could suck an errant vessel in that never saw it,
shred some innocent pleasure boater stem to stern
and spit him back while the tug's small crew went about
their evening business, drinking coffee, watching the VCR,

and the captain flicked his searchlight over the shoreline,
picking out the green marker right where he knew it was.
it's happened. it'll happen again. it could happen
to you, cruising at night away from your dock or
out of some small tributary, the great, dark, unlit mass

of the river ahead, your head filled with the whine
of your own I/Os, the last thing you ever hear or know
before you find yourself inside the high-walled canyon
of the barges. they're on their way upriver, after coal.
maybe at wheeling a deckhand'll find something splintered,

wedged between two barges, not a tree this once. maybe
he'll even know what it is, maybe recall some momentary

shudder in last night's passage, while he was dealing out
a hand of euchre, as if an engine skipped one heartbeat
and he saw the next day's work laid out for him. maybe not.

near death

—for Juanita Garciagodoy

in the old woman's dream the dog
she hadn't fed, wouldn't let in the house,
refused to help her cross the last river.
"fuck off, old woman," he barked,
"i don't owe you
anything"—and wagged his tail
and walked away like a shopkeeper
who sees you can't afford his goods.
"please," she called after him,
her fingers going brittle as frost,
"i can't cross without you,
i'll be stuck on this shore forever
among these raggedy *animas en peña.*"
the arch in his back as he strolled off
said "not my problem," and she couldn't,
really, argue with that,
though maybe, she thought, she didn't
have to make this crossing now
and as long as she could still smell
the beans and tortillas frying
she could find her way back home
and ponder this business of dogs awhile.
and maybe when she had it all figured out
and knew enough to accidentally knock
some scraps off the kitchen counter
she could even get a little better
at this dying.
but it would take years
and many, many dogs.

Life after all is fair; ultimately it breaks everybody's heart.
—Rachel Maddux, *Communication*

here's this land so flat the rain it can't soak up
just puddles where it falls. on either side of the interstate

life goes on with no horizon except the vague grey wall
the fog constructs today, behind which people even older than

myself might be sitting down to lunch now. i wonder why.
can there be sustenance here? between plowed-under cornfields

and the lay-offs at the caterpillar factory? it's all so
thin, as if the winter sky's come down and pressed

this land so flat the rain it can't soak up just puddles
where it falls. a film of water on a film of earth.

you can't slip the skin off a boiled new potato
any slicker than how it all slides away here. believe me,

there's nothing we can do to keep anything from happening:
the earth compresses and releases at its own rate:

no sense calling that breathing. i knew someone
who really did see angels once; they danced across a field

of purple clover and kept her going for twenty years or so
until the gin waltzed in. now it's work, work, work.

look at this thin strip of light we slide along at sixty
. . . sixty something. years or miles per hour, what

truth or sense there is spread out on either side like fog
along a land so flat the rain it can't soak up just

puddles where it falls. we look at it. it looks back at us.
this is how we know ourselves. that is how we know the world.

called me away at last from his second wife
with something sudden i couldn't quite translate
about the man he'd worked with all his life

whose famous integrity lay hidden from us here,
rolled up somewhere where we couldn't find it
like a pair of socks stuffed in a stone drawer.

already my father, too, had begun to fold
himself up with his sister and brother
into the little laundry baskets of the dead.

what a season that was! in ninety degrees
of heat and loss i walked in every little shade
while my father never even noticed the sun.

"one more time," i think he said, wading away
hip-deep into that granite lake, or maybe
it was "no more time," the hollow in his elbow

come to tug my own hand back. we stood, bent
beneath an august sun, to stare at the reserved
berths already made up between his parents

and the wife who'd mothered me. what a season
that was! what stone heat on a stone day!
i only wanted to know where my own mother lay,

but "why?" was the only thing that he would say,
or maybe it was "who?" or "cry" or "way": some
gutteral ghost-tongue phrase of his that said

only stone things in its stone world.

bad weather

no one's ever explained to me why the red oaks
save half their leaves to drop in spring:
that seems like such a bad, make-work idea
like cleaning out the garage, that litter-box
of rakes and rubble, bald tires, the broken-
handled shovel, rusted sled, disassembled bike,
the sand and grit the snow tires smuggle in.

we're wintering over too, most of us at least.
no explanation why. come spring, we'll drop
to our knees, wondering if it was a good idea
to outlast snow, fingering dirt still full
enough of frost to have risen from the grave.
the bulbs are rocks, our hands are rocks,
our crops are rocks and broken garden tools.

that springs like that don't seem a great idea
needs no explanation. you could drop them
from the cycle, for my money, hurry ahead
to the discontents of summer: crabgrass and
fairy rings, cedar-apple rust, the plague,
oak wilt, the busted mower and wind-burnt yew,
fevers, the bodies piling up on every side.

the military term *campaign* comes from the french
for countryside, where the armies wintered over
waiting for fighting weather. it always comes,
late-falling leaves littering the land like
flakes of rust, icy earth unready for its crop,
just being there a bad idea. no explanation
salvages the season where we drop.

in the tectonics of memory
the heavy plates of the past
slide up over the present
like a great continent coming ashore:
this is how mountains are made,
and who can cross them?
but listen: whole populations
live there, people you know!
it's not like you won't be recognized,
welcomed, fed: look who's come home!
the earth enfolds and shapes us.
how could it ever be otherwise?
and what is there to go back to?
here, it's like the world
has become young again: cliffs
steeper, streams swifter,
the wild rose finding its meadow
for the first time, so much
to be done and suddenly
all the time in the world.

II. HOLY WARS

holy wars (1944)

—for michael s. harper

1.

crammed against my adolescent will into the stuffy autumnal
box of cincinnati's sweaty, moorish plum street temple,
just across the street from the gothic fright of city hall
and hung on the edge of the west end ghetto its prosperous
people had long since bought their suburban way well out of
(though theirs were the names scrawled on its tenement deeds),

i only survived those deadly, hot, high holy days with a gun
cradled in my imagination. while the other guys drifted away
into sex or football, i huddled in the balcony of my mind
against a stone pillar at the very back of the choir loft
and picked those overdressed jews off one by one: there, there,
there, in the last days of the war, like woodchucks, with glee.

it was not my finest moment (though that's the way it happened
every holiday for years). there was nothing political to it:
i was hardly the young nazi, the dispossessed ghetto dweller.
it was merely the random violence of the imagination at play,
but what terrible play it was that i played out from the wooden
bench where the hand of the rabbi gently raised and lowered

the whole congregation, who had no idea that the kaddish
they chanted at the end of that long morning was for themselves
or that the benediction he finally said was for all my dead.

2.

later that fall for reasons i can't recall slender henry brown
and i wrestled each other to the gym floor. strangest of all,
for the first time in my own underweight life i ended up on top.

but looking down on henry brown's dark face i suddenly couldn't
imagine what i was doing there, what this brown boy i barely knew
was doing beneath me, looking up with eyes as amazed as mine.

i rolled away, sprawled on my own back on the wooden floor,
arms out, gasping. what a strange war! when was i recruited?
"things began to fall apart," you tell me now, "when jews

decided they were white people." it's an old story, of course,
this hand-me-down life, the ineradicable stink of the ghetto
still in my grandmother's house: but not in our neighborhood

where one day a week the *schvartze* ladies descended from buses
like migrant workers, spreading out with their shopping bags
across the neat suburban streets, performing their alchemy

of polished silver and starched white shirts until it grew dark
and men in battered buicks waited outside to drive them back
into the same crowded rooms our parents had been conceived in.

henry! when i sat up, head still spinning, you were already
gone: back, i suppose, like the boys who'd gathered around us,
into whatever games we'd been playing. i don't remember:

it was school: the games we played were the games we were
told to play. we were shy with each other. we said nothing.
gradually, like old shirts, we faded from each other's life.

3.

november then, and the year turning on its dark axis turning
the family in upon itself: my mother and i in the kitchen
in the early thanksgiving dusk watching our faces emerge
in the window over the sink, wet as the window with the sweat
of dishwater steam, dark as darkening evening behind the pane,
and some old uncle laughing at us, "sweating like *schvartzes*"
over the yam-sticky dishes and the greasy-lipped glasses
because rosa'd said she had to do for her own family today.

so did we all: it was a long day and the war was almost over
for now: paris free, rome free, the heavy adults snoozing
in the living room like cartoon characters with their shoes off
and newspapers spread over their faces, only the terrible pots
left to scrub and the spills for rosa to get out of the carpet
tomorrow and the camps, the camps that no one quite believed,
still to be liberated, no one understanding yet, no, not even
when the photographs began to appear in those same newspapers,

how that, too, was a middle passage, that mid-century crossing,
all those millions cast overboard, spoiled cargo, their bones
a white carpet spread across the dark sea of europe like
that wide white road of bones that paves the atlantic's floor,
and those who survived the crossings, rising from steamy seas,
and those who were there, exhausted, to help them ashore
and we who would come after, seeing our own faces mirrored
darkly in theirs, knowing their crossing our crossing . . .

and if i'd looked up just then i might have seen rosa with
her hands in the same dishwater, doing for her own family,
her small face, weary, tight, the way she looked coming up
the basement steps at the end of the day with mop and bucket,
there in the night-mirrored window, sweaty, above the sink,

right in between my mother's, who couldn't see her, and mine.
but "go," my mother said, "it's late, we're finished, we'll
leave the pots to soak overnight, for rosa." and i was gone.

i woke up late late in the twentieth century
and walked outside to snatch my morning paper
off the scorched lawn before it burst into flames,
the heat hammering me to my own concrete steps.
an oven, i thought (or cliché thought for me,
righter than rain), it's a fuckin' oven out here.

true, there are no words for times like these:
in the long dark, i remember, i was trying to
swim up to consciousness, but there's no swimming
in this. the paper only tells me that the worst
that can happen has already happened. and worse:
that i was witness. and what can i say to that?

the failure of language is the failure of knowledge.
quietly i slept, like a child. (i *was* a child.)
the news came and went, some in the paper, some not.
and i was right, there *were* ovens out there, but i
know nothing of them. their smoke is all the speech
i can bear. but i have to try: to say something,

or i'll never know what it is to be human. no,
i'll never even know what it is to be a horse:
to haul the cartloads of bodies to the lime pits
day in, day out, till i stumble too many times
and look up, at last, into the barrel of a gun,
still at a loss for words, always at a loss for words.

i wish i knew america better

there's a zuni fetish black bear peering over the edge
of my monitor right now as if standing on a mesa
scanning the brown desert of my desk below:

a slender turquoise arrow pierces it to the heart
of an america i wish i knew better: the one you can't see
from thirty thousand feet, the one i've slid right by

in all the million miles i've driven on its blood-slicked
highways. i wish i knew america better: the famous
back yards on the other side of the tracks waving

their laundry as the trains hurry by, ancient pontiacs
settling deeper into the sands of the dry wash,
indian-head hood ornaments still tipping their chins

up, just the way my grandmother used to cock her head
for every photograph: call it pride. i remember
the fires that smoldered perpetually in the city dumps

where the acrid old men lived: i remember my ignorance.
i knelt on the forest trail to hold the young dog
back from the black bear's furry grip until it turned

and sauntered away as if to say, you don't know me.
there are men and women just like that. i wish
i knew america better. aside from corn there's nothing

in all those fields i've driven by that i can identify.
o city boy, city boy, what are you doing in this
country? is there someone around who adores that feedlot

stink? who hungers for tenement hallways papered
with the brown stench of fat meat, old oil? someone
whose eyes water those coal-stained appalachian

hollows? once upon a time it was possible to smell
precisely when and where you were; now they've outlawed
the autumn leaf. my nose can still decipher the bitter

flavor of the black bear's recent passage, but
if something's burning, it'd better be making something
else go: that's an america i do know. nevertheless,

ignorance is a short leg: you walk in circles,
wearing a track deeper and deeper into your one life
until that tidy cookie-cutter hole you've dug yourself

becomes your grave and everything you never knew
is pitching its tents, banging up its chipboard houses,
on that mound of dirt above your head, never even looking

at you, not even aware you're down below: someone
who once wished he knew america better, who lifted his chin
in the family tradition, sniffed the air, not like a bear

swaying its heavy, knowledgeable head through the forest
dark, but like a child, calling "come out, come out,
wherever you are": listening to the night, smelling it,

holding my breath: thinking of an america i wish i knew.

optical illusions

these optical illusions in the woods that make a blackened stump
look like a bear or, further off, a moose, especially
when you're puffing up a rugged trail and get that sudden glimpse
through a stand of birches or shadowed under jack pines,
remind you what the world consists of: surprise, amazement, then
that quick recalculation of your chances for survival
the unexpected always tests you on, even when there's really no
surprise at all as those imagined beasts shouldn't be
since it's, after all—if they'd been truly there—their woods or
even in their absence, yes, their ownership still figures
in your figuring since for all the quick relief that follows your
first panic there could be a real bear berrying behind
that blackened stump or a moose headed down that path with nothing,
including you, to fear. in other words there are no real
illusions. that blue toyota that came around the hairpin curve
on highway 1 last sunday evening at sixty miles an hour
on my side of the road was every bit as real as the gunfire that
raked my dreams the night before, and i did right to
dodge them both though i'm still not sure how i got out of either
one alive. not by being ready, that's for sure; maybe
by taking whatever happened at face value. those optical illusions
own the world because they might be real even when you
know they're not. take love, for example, far rarer than any moose
you ever even thought you saw, but you wouldn't miss
the chance that what you felt just might be the real thing this time,
so you stand there gaping at a shadow between the pines,
remetamorphosing daphne in your mind out of this cloudcast or that
broken branch and all the while some sharp-clawed bear's
lumbering up the trail behind you, no optical illusion: like love,
you never saw it coming. the way it always happens,
the real illusion slashing at your backside's what you never even
didn't think you saw: that overloaded logging truck

tailgating me down twenty twisting miles of highway 1 while i
was busy daydreaming a blue toyota's graceful flight
into a moosey bog. how the heart leaps when you suddenly look up
to see what fills your rearview mirror! and won't go
away. flicks its bright lights on as soon as darkness falls. wants
the road. you don't even dare slow down to find a niche
to pull off in. maybe doesn't even see you're there. or takes you
for an optical illusion. you won't be anything until
the world, speeding down its usual winding road, rolls right over you.

the man in the moon

white-faced, white-suited, as big as the full moon in the tropical sky
i've just dropped out of, wheezy and confident as sidney greenstreet
in *the maltese falcon,* the fat man rolls my way across the waiting room

of the small airport in south india. it is 1966. in a sky of black faces
i have never seen anything whiter than this. it is the moon, the moon
in its tropical cotton and straw, wavering my way in its erratic orbit,

white jacket flapping, and i feel myself being drawn up into its lunatic
gravity. see how it parts the dark heavens between us! how even at dawn
it beams with the pleasure of its fullness! how to the stranger i am it

announces itself in its own reflected glare, with moony arms spread wide
and moony paw and cratered moony grin, as the head jew of cochin.

*

it's the being known i always battle. what was i wearing, a yellow star?
'bruder!' 'landsman!' how do they always know you, wherever you are?
up all night on the long flight east, i hardly knew myself for what i was.

was i this white? as small as me but beautiful and black the indian men
and women swirled like spiral galaxies in corners of the waiting room,
rippling from his passage, the pale, disturbing perturbations of the moon.

this is the way the cosmos curves, i guess, space in its curious symmetries
bending around some lump of the familiar, small objects caught and bound
by forces they neither like nor understand. i took a few steps back, but

our orbits were fixed by then. for a year we circled each other. he was
a decent, generous man. a sometime host and help, never quite a friend.

★

a quarter century old now, too white to say it fades, the memory . . .
wanes. occasionally, though, on clear summer nights when the full moon
washes most of the stars from the sky and there's an almost tropical smell

to even these northern woods, when the birch and balsam and pine exhale
their own exotic perfumes—i was a stranger here, too, 25 years ago—
i remember that huge, pale, round-faced, white-suited man in the moon

looming suddenly over me, arms spread wide, trying to gather me up in
his ancient tidal surge. did i travel halfway around the world for that?
the stranger i was was the stranger i wanted to be. leave me alone,

i wanted to cry, even as i shook his hand. around us the dark, bright
faces sparkled. why was he even there? fact: it was his world, too:
there'd been jews in cochin for a thousand years. but he hung, in my

black sky, like a terrible white sign: they know you wherever you are.

that day

suppose, at last, they come for you, as you always knew they would:
not in the dead of night--no need for that--but on some rainy afternoon
when you're just hanging around in your ratty grey sweats, wondering
if it's worth the trouble to light a little fire to take the chill off.
you know what they want but you don't even hear what they're saying,
all you hear is the voice of your long-dead father from your childhood
warning you to watch out, telling you they're everywhere out to get you.
so all your life you've watched, looking both ways at every intersection,
surviving all your crossings, proving him wrong, outliving his worst fears.
but you're his age now, and it's as if he's come back to get you at last.
these uniforms mean nothing. they drag you out the door with his strength,
toss you lightly into the back of the truck. behind you the furnace
clicks on, whispering fatherly advice through every room. the rain
snickers knowingly in the open doorway. the truck is full of fathers
like yourself, who did not listen, who did not warn their own children,
who are shivering in old t-shirts and bathrobes, mis-buttoned shirts.
it was one of those saturdays when nothing happens. a ball game on tv.
yardwork if the rain lets up. a nap. the dream you always feared:
the gun butts banging at the door again, the voice that says i told you so.

the sidewalk's no place to bend over and tie your shoes:
baring your back to the world like that picks your own locks
and you're a statistic maybe a day or two ahead of schedule,
if that matters when all the odds are with the shooters, with
the lovers and drinkers and looters, when every time you lay
your hand down on the counter someone slips some solid steel
into your palm. and there's plenty to fear without people.
think of those killer asteroids like bright blue flowers
a mile wide dotting the meadows above us, nodding earthward
as the wind of our passage moves over them, each terratropic
blossom a reminder that if the heavens bend toward us it's
not necessarily a blessing. check it out with the dinosaurs
if you think this sounds like fun. we could look up one day
into the eye of a bright flower, rays spread across the sky
like angels descending, and all the knives in the streets
quietly fold themselves up and the gun hands drop—though
whether in relief or terror we'll never know. for the first
time in years you'll signal your turn pulling off the freeway,
look for a legal spot to show how good you've finally gotten
at parallel parking, even remember a quarter for the meter
before you get out to stand on the sidewalk with all the rest
of us. there's always something, you say, about endings,
and someone else says, the sky is not falling but blooming.

crystal night

the antique wineglass the sexy little grad student drained
in one quick gulp and chunked like a rock into the fireplace
as we sat on the floor finishing the three curries i'd cooked
exploded in the hard flames like that whole first november
of my madness. into what wild hands had the world cast me?
"look," she said, "what i can do," upending herself suddenly
between our greasy plates, kicking herself into a headstand
and my wineglass, this time, into a little arc beside my knee,
its thin stem cracking and the dark, expensive wine bleeding
into the carpet. i knew what she could do: it was november
already, i'd lived in a dark haze all year, neither rain nor
snow, knowing well the world would never be the same again.
heavy as a casket, she eased herself down into my lap, saying,
"take off your belt now, i won't be hurt." i took it off.

coming downstairs, later, i found the fire dead, the night
with its hands still wrapped around the throat of the world,
the streetlight glinting fiercely through the shattered snow,
shards of wineglass bright as starlight on the icy hearth,
everything almost beautiful, even the curled snake of my belt
asleep or dead in the center of the room: all the nothing
that hadn't changed. it was still november, mad november,
the snow, even as i watched, easing itself back into a cold
november rain, part ice, part snow, glassy under streetlights,
brittle on the fractured sidewalks, like some broken window
letting its cold novembers in forever, and i understood, now,
nothing: not her, asleep in her brutal bones above, not
mad november's icy image caught in every awful piece of glass
or how i'd bend, all day, to sweep the thousand fragments up.

i'd like to think that snowfall has no other meanings, that
a fine compound word harnessed to what the skies are doing
right now has all the weight it needs to pull, that
once it's dragged me to the window to see the white
that's shutting down the world, that's enough, and that
if it slides off the roof and buries me up to my neck
while i'm shoveling the driveway, that's enough, too, more
than enough, i'd say, but still just snowfall: "snowfall":
you can't rearrange the letters to spell "purity" or "death"
and even if you bulk it up to blizzard strength, like
this one threatens to do, close the highways, shut down
the airport, the change is quantitative, not qualitative,
flat as the way that last line slips on the ice, goes down
moaning but, really, not trying to make anything of it,
just grateful for the snow that eases the pain of the fall.

the god that isn't is just like the god that is—absent,
inarticulate, confused: so when i tell you about this
snowfall, give me a shovel, not some sly, pitying smile
as if i didn't understand what i was saying. better yet,
dig in yourself, see if beneath these ten or twelve wet,
white inches you can help me find the proof concrete,
the syllogism perfect and obtuse: a cleared drive's
the sure way out, and once we've shoveled, here we go,
but only as far as the street that hasn't been plowed,
and when it is, the beautiful driveway's blocked again.
a heart attack's the most adult response to the snowfall
we loved as a child: it says a lifefull. it speaks
to how the world compounds itself: snowstorm, snowman,
snowdrift, snowbank, snowbound, snowplow, snowbird.
that's what's there, white for a while and all you see.
take that away, bud, and there's only shit to shovel.

street scene

Life grinds/on

—*Pablo Neruda,* "Things Breaking"

that fellow walking up the street with a gun in his head
could be me—but he isn't, and i don't know why:
the self's such a trifling thing to bring the price it does
in this market: shoddy domestic goods always
breaking down, the import market looking better every day,
the bargaining so violent. social psychologists
tell me the self's an impossible control group, the quantum
of stupidity the same regardless of any variables.
and we thought it was change we had to arm ourselves against.
if i crossed to the other side would i meet myself
coming and going? left side, right side: the brain keeps
talking to itself as if someone's listening. "you
could turn around and go home," it says (*i'm* listening!),
"but that's mostly dirty dishes." and cold, greasy
water, don't i know it. and the streets? supposing he steps
into a doorway and i hear the click in his mind
as he snaps the safety off. the headstones in the cemetery
are sitting up, waiting to see if i'll join them,
but there's no rush, they already know i'm on their side,
and everyone else is ignoring the scene, head down,
studying the sidewalk as if it had turned into gravy, critics,
all of them, brooding on lumps and saturated fats
as if they'd just strolled into the end of *Gone With The Wind*.
tomorrow. oh, dear. it won't do any good, but
i suppose i'll be better prepared. don't think i think this
is *High Noon,* either. but if you do put a gun
in my hand, please make sure it's turned the right way.

all freight, the sudden trains that uncouple my passage home
like flash floods, stranding me in these winter afternoon rains
counting carloads of lumber, flatcars of heavy equipment, sealed
boxcars headed out of the city, cities themselves, miles long and
full of industry, but with only a grim mayor at the throttle
and a handful of sleepy maintenance workers for inhabitants:
where have all the passengers, all the rightful citizens, gone?

in 1940, in the dazed center of my childhood and the last year
before the war—our war—we watched my suited, suitcased father
descend the tiled concourse to board "the james whitcomb riley"
at cincinnati's brand-new, brassy, domed and cavernous, art-
decoed union terminal with its floor-to-ceiling mosaics of labor
and industry. almost empty even then, it echoed with the hard
departures of newstands, shoeshine boys, our own hurried heels
on the marble floors. then it was troop trains, troop trains,
all troop trains: the long, thrilling, khaki freight of the war.

but what did we know of trains then? of industrious engineers
hauling their boxcars of battered freight across the cavernous
wastes of europe to stoke the engines of empire like so much
kindling? of winters thick with the smoke of coal and flesh?
no wonder we take to the air now, or sit in our cars, dreaming,
while the long cities of the dead roll by. somewhere, even then,
there must have been a citizen stopped at a level crossing on a
winter day just like this, motor turned off to save the precious
fuel, counting the rattling box cars, thick with the nostalgia
only these cold rains can bring, ignorant, dreaming of trains.

III. HURRY BACK

it's hard work, friends, trying to stitch this raggedy earth
into a wearable shirt. by the time i get it to fit it'll only be fit
to bury me in. ok, but i'd like someone to admire my handiwork
a day or so before then, even with a lie. just say it

looks good on me. i know one sleeve's longer than the other,
so what? it still holds me together, which is all i ever asked of clothes.
and it's mine, wearable and wearing, nothing fashionable or clever,
only what i've needled my fingers with, worked for, chose.

so who'll tell me now it's time to rest awhile? no more of that
'let us go then, you and i. . . .' i'd like to just sit here
a bit, a weary fan, applauding the polluted skies for the gorgeous sunset,
remembering how at izzy's they used to rush you through your

corned beef, half a dozen people waiting for your seat and then izzy
himself crying 'hurry back' while he made the register ring.
they want too much of you and all at once, which is why we have this zany
passion for the boundlessness of baseball, where no inning

ever has to end or be the last. imagine a game that goes on forever
at its own pace, forever slowing as the players age, a tailor
in the dugout stitching up the tattered uniforms, reliever
on the mound, batter at the plate, forever panting and forever . . .

but what do i know? convenience stores are hemming in my neighborhood,
places with names like kwik stop and hurry back that instruct
you to leave your motor running en route to the good
life. but if a quick quart of two percent's what truth's come to, we're fucked,

friends, and might as well just grab the first shabby chemise
that slides off the rack and find our places in that old procession
of animals and people shuffling dumbly along to the sacrifice,
the steady, dependable multitude: their knowledge, their desolation.

1944: prokofiev is hiding out in the urals with the kirov
ballet, writing his *cinderella,* and i am twelve years old
and have just, in the midst of a soft summer twilight game
of kick-the-can, fallen in love, for the first time, with
the only girl i ever meet who can outrun me. dear prokofiev,
how are these things possible in the midst of such carnage?
granted that the german army is already on the run and that
i will never catch up with that speedy little blond for even
the few moments i need to tell her that i'm in love with her,
we still need to ask how, in the midst of this holocaust,
we dare to dream of these princesses in flight at midnight.

1984: the royal ballet is dancing *cinderella* at covent garden
and i am in love again, with the only woman i have ever met
who can outrun me while standing in the same place. i know
i'll never catch up with her but i'm running as fast as i can.
maybe it's the flight that enchants us: i have just watched
the ballerina take off like doctor j, fifteen feet from the
basket, do one full turn, switch hands, slam dunk, and float
down to the earth again precisely when and where she wants.
it doesn't seem possible for a human being to do such a thing
and yet i myself am here to say that i've just seen it done.
the carnage, of course, continues. the same question remains
but prokofiev is no longer here to help. he did, however, say,
'it's important that *cinderella* be as danceable as possible.'
listen to prokofiev. it is midnight. never forget the dancing.

the language of flowers

we didn't have the names for many flowers back then:
just the long-stemmed roses that my father'd better
send my mother twice a year and the white gardenia
wrist corsages for our dance dates, white carnation
boutonnieres for us; the dying zinnias of my mother's
one attempt at gardening; hydrangea, maybe, maybe not,
in a neighbor's yard; now and then on some friend's
parents' polished maple dinner table a garish bird of
paradise cocked halfway over as if in awful pain; and,
just once, an orchid, though it didn't do me any good.

but it was the depression and its aftermath, the war,
when everything, including, one might imagine, flowers,
went to help the "effort," though there were always
dandelions that our neighbor picked for salad greens
and a tidy lawn (while ours stayed pocked with yellow
till we plucked the puffballs, swung them high, and
watched them drop their paratroops behind his lines).
and if my little brother on his way home from school
pulled up a handful of white clover for our mother,
that was both something amazing and something we had

some names for: but nothing like what i can see now
even along the roadside near my house ever since i
learned that yellow-petaled daisy-like configuration
with the darker center was called a black-eyed susan,
that turtle-headed flower down in the drainage ditch,
a turtlehead, and that tall and purple-tinged umbel
on the slope behind it, joe pye weed. oh the wonder
of these names. who was joe pye? could anything be
more right than "umbel?" why "susan," rather than
"nancy" or "michael?" of course the turtleheads are

rising out of the water! names take you by the hand
and walk you down a forest path you walked a hundred
times before, not seeing the bunchberries though it's

spring and they're everywhere, white as snow against
the green, not seeing cow parsnip right there at your
own eye level, or orange hawkweed, or the well-named
lovely one-flowered wintergreen. oh wordless was i
born, and wordless did i grow, ignorant of the real
name for those red roses my father sent, ignorant of
the names i had to learn to learn the names for love.

wintering over at the end of the century

1.

bringing the plants inside that flourished
all summer long on the front porch i sense
a little of what hades might have felt
welcoming reluctant persephone back home:
that sunwarmed skin, that yellow scent
of wildflowers on her breath, in her hair,
and, yes, the dark weight of the season
slowing her step as she enters this world.

2.

what will we do for light in here? where
shall the crotons go? the ferns, ivies,
jade and spider plants? on what window
sill will the african violets still flower,
the cyclamen that bloomed all summer long?
i do this job like a jailer, joylessly,
my hands filthy, smelling of cold dirt
and damp, of necessary things done badly.

3.

night edges in on us from both directions
as this corner of the earth turns its face
from the sun. yes, the same old things
go on, but they begin and end in the dark.
some call that a blessing and we know why.
persephone herself will soon grow as pale
as a dieffenbachia leaf starved for light,
and we will pale, too, in time, in time.

4.

yet there's a green candle sputtering up
from every clay or plastic pot i carry in,
and one by one as i set this pot here and
that one there the darkening rooms take on
a glow they never had before. all summer
long i think, ignorant as geraniums, we
must have been preparing for this moment:
when the last begonias would move inside

with us to take up their annual, wintery
residence on some barren shelf or table,
a sudden, green, and tropical reminder of
where they've been, and who and where we are.

almost always

birds feeding on the highway almost always
fly up in time, but you, when you come over
the rise at sixty five with a semi on your tail,
where will you go? the etiquette of the road
says you can leave the table anytime you want,
anytime you feel the world bearing down on you
too heavily, but you've got to have somewhere to go.
people die from not knowing where to go next,
from slow reaction time and two-lane blacktop gluttony,
in their fragile vehicles of feather and bone.

so talk to yourself, to your foot on the brake if you
must, but make it quick or you'll have a back seat
full of truck and never know the scatter and squawk
of a flock of blackbirds on the road's dark track.
remember: birds feeding on the highway almost
always fly up in time. they know some things
you don't: hunger for the road's a relative thing,
there are other directions than straight ahead,
it pays to have an eye on each side of your head.

so: that semi and you and the birds: everything
either behind you or before you as you come up
over the rise on this winding two-lane blacktop
country road at ten miles over the speed limit,
just the way you've traveled all your life, only
slightly out of control, wondering if it's true,
wondering if it's really true that birds feeding
on the highway almost always fly up in time.

many people go through life feeling
a shadow is stalking them, a cloak they didn't put on
and can't take off, a pair of heavy wings . . .
a movement in the bathroom mirror like a cloud
brushing across the face of the sun but quick
when they turn the world still dazzles them
even though they've closed the bathroom door behind them,
and they have to go on living as if
there were nothing there, too embarrassed to ask
their friends, when they're sitting in a restaurant,
to see what sort of thing's pulled up a chair behind them.

and they're not crazy, either. i envy them,
who spend my days with the shadow out in front of me,
a chase car criss-crossing the countryside
in and out of the shadow of a hot-air balloon,
always a cornfield, a river, sometimes a little hill
between me and where i have to be, always
the candy-striped globe dazzling the sky above me
while i track the shadow skipping away
from me over the rooftops, the haystacks, into the woods.

oh shadow, shadow, how i skid around the curves!
the u-turns i make at crowded intersections!
and it's not even you i want, shadow, but the whole
brilliant balloon that stuns the sky like a sun above me.

small pleasures

here, we take our pleasures small: a february afternoon
when the sun still lingers, just past five, on our side
of the horizon, a purple sweater we'll recall forever
as the greatest bargain of the after-christmas sale—
but rarely wear, the first frail robin of a distant spring
skipping across the lawn in a flurry of snow and concern.

there's not much that we can't make something of: the pen
with puppy teeth marks on its cap becomes a poem, the note
you left beneath my pillow when you left becomes a charm
(confusing, though: against departures or against return?),
the dustball in the corner of a dream becomes a storm of
half-remembered houses, a blizzard of badly-slept-in rooms

in which the only thing to wait all night for was the sun
chinning its goofy self on the snowy roof across the street
as if it were something special, some vaudeville routine
gone totally out of fashion, but still . . . it's dawn!
and we're still here! just small, pale wintry things,
but never done with what we're done with till we're done.

against dreaming

nambé: 17 september 1993

in morning sunlight, beneath the grapevine dangling from the tin
porch roof and bouncing with the coming and going of sparrows
in their quick hunger for its hard little purple fruits,
i try to reassemble last night's dream, sensuous and desperate:
a woman's body, lost shoes, one of our dogs in trouble
who was all i managed to cope with while everything else
went its own odd way. but it's like a visit to the doctor
where all i remember is what it felt like, not what it was.
isn't that the wrong way around? doesn't content count?
are feelings content? i was crying, yes, but not out loud,
not like this chorus of magpies rattling the cottonwoods,
defying dreams, like my father who arrived at the very end,
alive again, helpful, yes, but impatient: get on with it,
he didn't have to say. the world always snaps get on with it!
and then surprises you with a wide-winged blue day like this:
and who can resist it? it's a bad dream that can hold itself
together against all this: flutter in the arbor, the real dog
asleep in early sunlight, sparkle of water through the latilla
fence, cat on the old wood railing, quiet, quiet, two trucks
hissing down the dirt road, a whisper of wings. i know
you're sleeping. i know i'm awake. i know i'm not dreaming.

starlight, starbright . . .

we're always saying goodbye to the universe: look up:
you'll never see anything leaving you faster than that.
look down, look over here: ditto. light is light.
everything's light, waving the fastest farewells,

"goodby, goodbye" from the very beginning: bang!
(who dunnit?) and gone: you won't catch me. and now
we see it in the stars, their hundred-thousand-year-agos:
if only we could see our own pasts as clearly as that!

and yet they're out there somewhere: fizzling, you bet,
but still hurrying away from us at the same crazy speed
we lived them, packets of spent energy still recklessly
spending themselves across the void. and we wonder:

what would happen if they met out there somewhere, yours
and mine? what restless dreams in that! how we toss
in our sleep like coins, heads for hope, tails for despair,
never knowing which side will turn up in the morning,

not even knowing which side it makes sense to wish for.

the children all grown and gone now it surprises me,
out walking the dog alone, to see some young father
driving one of his kids, the son i think, off to,
maybe, a music lesson. do parents still do that?
even on my street? dumb questions, i know, almost
like asking if they still eat breakfast, go to school,
but isn't it amazing to think that things i once did
people still do, as if to say, yeah, there's something
to all that? and the kid had his elbow out the window
and was whistling as they drove past me, a sure sign
that he knew this was something well worth doing, so

maybe i'm the only one who wonders what's with all this
repetition: those new millions out there every year
learning to bunt or play the oboe, learning body parts
and yardwork and the colors of the alphabet, learning
it all over again as if this hasn't been done millions
of times before and they won't grow up to drive their
daughters and sons off to hockey rinks and pet stores
and whatever the shopping mall, the old arcade that is,
downtown, you know, turns into twenty years from now.
but then, just before i take the dog back in the house

and put his evening feeding out, as i do this same time
every day, i hear the little girl across the street say
to her friend, 'if i could have anything i want, i'd want
a cookie tree in my back yard,' and i hear the sound of
something ripping, probably just another northwest jet
in its scheduled ascent splitting apart the neighborhood
sky above me, yeah, i'm sure that's all it is, what with

the girls playing in the bushes where i can't even see
them, but i hear them giggling and then i hear it again,
the sound the earth makes when something new tears free,
the sound that spring would make on a time-lapse tape of
something bursting through, some fern or flower or tree.

happiness

for janet: 2 october 1992

even though we fear horses and have no use for monarchy,
when the king on his fat horse casts his eye over the crowd
and lowers his smile on us, we study our shoes and smile.
what else is there to do? a brush with joy is like that:
just give the word and we'll grovel. but it's annoying,
too: we were only on our way to the shoe repair shop,
your humble servant of the quotidian, regal processions
not even the last thing on our mind, what with democracies
bleeding to be born everywhere these days. oh politics,
we were thinking, mired in the waiting mob, scraping our
boots on the curb, wondering whether we'd bother to vote
for the county commissioner next month: all the romance
gone with weak-headed kings and demented queens, the petty
scramble for the empty throne. and then, suddenly, there!
just when we were realizing how it's always the chancellor
of the exchequer, whatever it's called, there's always one,
neither elected nor inherited, that the whole enterprise
turns on; just when we noticed that even the moccasins we
were wearing needed to be restitched; just when we felt
in the late afternoon of an october day that first autumnal
easterly creaking down the street like some old gentleman
loving twilight but hating to see the summer sun go down:
there, in that ragged procession, that sudden pain in the
aspirations of getting the day's last errands run . . .
a fat white horse . . . an ermined king . . . a smile!

the search for a unified theory

see that pair of fine white lines easing into one
that divides the sky precisely in half as it feathers
out across the palest blue? at those altitudes it's
always winter. whatever we spew out's crystallized
and beautiful, a distant, brief, unlivable geometry,
brittle as the china glittering on the dinner table
just before the guests arrive, before the drip-drip
of candle wax and conversation, the first red stains
of cabernet on lace, that fractal, fractured image
of the evening as it ought to be: people in summer
clothing lounging against the grip of straight-backed
chairs, chickadees and goldfinches quickly on and off
the feeder's rigid metal pegs, those dogs lingering
under the table for whatever random scraps might fall
and a rumor, only, of thunderheads building out west:

'symmetry,' says the architect, spreading his wings
across the stage of the new concert hall, 'is the enemy
of music.' his beautiful, crooked smile says 'listen.'
it's the eddy, not the onrush, draws you in. water's
more often than not the answer, whatever the question.
the end is never in the beginning: not one word about
the gulf of mexico spills from lake itasca's outlet.
a few boulders here, a little continental uplift there:
who knows? this is the song we should all be singing:
one like the all-too-often-neglected cacophony of crows:
the one in which the sky itself disassembles bit by bit
every crystal construct we enact. we can navigate by
pre-copernican rules, and do, but planetary wobble's
the table with one short leg where we sit down to dine.

hummingbird-like the talk hovers on the edge of intimacy,
darts in, drinks quick and deep, then's gone—no, there,
on the twig's edge, waiting. . . . nothing's circular,
understand: even the 'o' in 'love' has pits and warts;
pushing it out of round's what makes it ours: so rejoice:
the bell curve lies about me, lies about you. nothing
says we can't reprise this dinner every wednesday night
at seven for the rest of our lives, same good company,
same menu, same good wine . . . except a skittery flight
of snowflakes this time, politics that, sudden silence
at a certain name, bird's eye twinkle of wit, a laugh,
a chorus of coughs, slosh of the overfilled water glass,
all the ungraph- and ungraspable flakes of the evening
that sift down over us, inside and out, each single one
a perfect hexagon, we think, as it seems about to settle
on our hands . . . then melts: and we're what's left:
dogs at our feet and our hands oddly angled in air, empty,
for the moment, and damp, and unsymmetrical, and here.

something amazing

in the home movie the kids (grown now) are clowning around
in the living room, mugging at the camera, ignorant
of the tornado pirouetting in the picture window behind them,
and though i plead with them to run it back and freeze
that frame, they're clowning around again right now in another
living room, complete with babies, paying no attention
to the past, no one listening to me even though it's my dream.
people just don't get it, do they: the storm that's
always brooding in the background while they're spreading
bologna sandwiches with mayo and making with the old
familial patter as if life really were a picnic. these kids!

somewhere beyond the borders of this waking dream, the dogs
racing through the tall weeds, a rabbit defending its burrow
against the predatory crow swaying in the top of the scrubby
boxelder tree, the horse at ease behind its electrified fence,
even the gaudy hot-air balloon drifting at a dignified pace
over the distant rise and out of sight—are all holding hands
in a conspiracy of the normal. what does it take to believe?
at night the sky turns greenish grey, the winds come rushing
out of every crooked corner of the house, all my sirens wail.

nothing prepares us for the fact that life goes on. where do
sayings like "let the dead bury their dead" come from
and what do they mean? i have studied ignorance every semester
for sixty years now, and i'm finally getting the idea.
if the lake chews noisily at the shoreline like the dog on her
bone though they could both be napping in the sunshine
on this windless day, i'm all in favor of it. bury me
with all my degrees under my folded hands: bachelor of dreams,
masters in melancholy, ph.d. in loss. there's nothing
here to understand: the big kids and the little ones get to
keep the birdfeeder full, the rest of us get to keep on dying.

that's my dream, anyway. and if it's my hands turning red
from adding food coloring to the hummingbirds' sugar water,
i don't want to hear about it. they've had a long flight
and need some easy living now. remember the chickadee winter?
how they came down in snowiest january to take the birdseed
right out of our hands? i thought i stood out on the deck,
my ungloved hands numbing, to take a photograph of that, but
i've turned my life upside down and i can't find it anywhere.
some days, even stupidity cries out in its sleep for evidence.

what's truly amazing is not the road crews laying fresh asphalt
in this summer heat as if the sky weren't falling in and
we really had somewhere to go but all the others bearing witness
to it: those grumps on the national transportation board,
the county commissioner's bedraggled staff, construction bidders,
architects, engineers, union secretaries, gravel loaders,
voters and bondholders and dump truck drivers and backhoe jockeys
and even the college kid sweating in the bright orange vest
and spinning her tall sign between STOP and SLOW while we all sit
in long lines of air-conditioned traffic explaining phenomena
of consciousness. i hope they get it done in time for the picnic.

quotidian

i want to think, when i see the sun come up these winter
mornings, that i'm seeing the sun come up: over the roof
next door, through the fat oak's lattice of rusty leaves,

over squirrels already busy at its base, frosted cars,
icy skin on the next door neighbor's concrete birdbath:
the real sun, that is, through whatever morning haze

the season brings: ground fog, thin miasma of my own slow
waking, dreams i've dragged along to the window like sleepy
children trailing stuffed animals, wondering what's so

important, why they had to get up to see some dopey, daily
thing. because, see, it rises in the face of all the earth's
uncalculated clutter, that systemic chaos that leads us

from what is to what is not. because it is what it is,
capable, in the right season, of calling forth the oily
iridescent crackle of the grackle's back or pigeon's neck

or rolling the dogs on their backs in the long spring grass.
because every slightly less belated winter morning it's there
again, not even on its own volition but caught in the wide,

encompassing, effortless arc of the absolute: like air,
like earth, the dirt we drag in the house on our shoes
and the clean carpet it clings to, black clumps of dog hair

in the corner, and your open book face down on the bedside
table, its pale yellow cover arching ever so slightly up
as if it, too, were only waiting to rise into my hands.